DOVER·THRIFT·EDITIONS

The Sea Gull

ANTON CHEKHOV

DOVER PUBLICATIONS, INC.
Mineola, New York

DOVER THRIFT EDITIONS

GENERAL EDITOR: PAUL NEGRI

Published in Canada by General Publishing Company, Ltd., 30 Lesmill Road, Don Mills, Toronto, Ontario.
Published in the United Kingdom by Constable and Company, Ltd., 3 The Lanchesters, 162–164 Fulham Palace Road, London W6 9ER.

Theatrical Rights

This Dover Thrift Edition may be used in its entirety, in adaptation, or in any other way for theatrical productions, professional and amateur, in the United States, without permission, fee, or acknowledgment. (This may not apply outside of the United States, as copyright conditions may vary.)

Bibliographical Note

This Dover edition, first published in 1999, is an unabridged republication of a standard edition. The Note was prepared specially for this edition.

Library of Congress Cataloging-in-Publication Data

Chekhov, Anton Pavlovich, 1860–1904.
    [Chaĭka. English]
    The sea gull / Anton Chekhov.
       p.   cm. — (Dover thrift editions)
    ISBN 0-486-40656-3 (pbk.)
    I. Title. II. Series.
PG3456.C5   1999
891.72'3—dc21
                                                  99-12248
                                                  CIP

Manufactured in the United States of America
Dover Publications, Inc., 31 East 2nd Street, Mineola, N.Y. 11501

Note

The great Russian dramatist and story writer Anton Pavlovich Chekhov (1860–1904) was a major figure in the development of modern drama. He began to write stories and plays while still a medical student at the University of Moscow. He received his degree in medicine in 1884, but practised little, choosing rather to pursue a literary career. His early successes were stories—mainly humorous—published in the papers and later in book form.

Chekhov's first major play, *Ivanov*, was produced in 1887, and was followed by the four works on which his reputation as a master playwright is based: *The Sea Gull, Uncle Vanya, The Three Sisters*, and *The Cherry Orchard*. *The Sea Gull*, Chekhov's second major play, was first produced in 1896, and due to a complete misunderstanding of the work by the director and actors was a dismal failure, prompting Chekhov to declare he would never write another play. Two years later, however, in a more sympathetic production at the Moscow Art Theater, the play was a resounding success and has remained enormously popular ever since. Its exploration of the themes of loneliness and alienation, combined with Chekhov's extraordinary ability to create real and compelling characters, have earned it a place as a major play in world literature.

Characters

IRINA ARKADINA, *an actress*
CONSTANTINE TREPLIEFF, *her son*
PETER SORIN, *her brother*
NINA ZARIETCHNAYA, *a young girl, the daughter of a rich landowner*
ILIA SHAMRAEFF, *the manager of* SORIN's *estate*
PAULINA, *his wife*
MASHA, *their daughter*
BORIS TRIGORIN, *an author*
EUGENE DORN, *a doctor*
SIMON MEDVIEDENKO, *a schoolmaster*
JACOB, *a workman*
A COOK
A MAIDSERVANT

The scene is laid on SORIN's *estate. Two years elapse between the third and fourth acts.*

ACT I

The scene is laid in the park on SORIN's *estate. A broad avenue of trees leads away from the audience toward a lake which lies lost in the depths of the park. The avenue is obstructed by a rough stage, temporarily erected for the performance of amateur theatricals, and which screens the lake from view. There is a dense growth of bushes to the left and right of the stage. A few chairs and a little table are placed in front of the stage. The sun has just set.* JACOB *and some other workmen are heard hammering and coughing on the stage behind the lowered curtain.*

MASHA *and* MEDVIEDENKO *come in from the left, returning from a walk.*

MEDVIEDENKO.   Why do you always wear mourning?

MASHA.   I dress in black to match my life. I am unhappy.

MEDVIEDENKO.   Why should you be unhappy? [*Thinking it over*] I don't understand it. You are healthy, and though your father is not rich, he has a good competency. My life is far harder than yours. I only have twenty-three roubles a month to live on, but I don't wear mourning.

[*They sit down.*

MASHA.   Happiness does not depend on riches; poor men are often happy.

MEDVIEDENKO.   In theory, yes, but not in reality. Take my case, for instance; my mother, my two sisters, my little brother and I must all live somehow on my salary of twenty-three roubles

1

a month. We have to eat and drink, I take it. You wouldn't have us go without tea and sugar, would you? Or tobacco? Answer me that, if you can.

MASHA.   [*Looking in the direction of the stage*] The play will soon begin.

MEDVIEDENKO.   Yes, Nina Zarietchnaya is going to act in Treplieff's play. They love one another, and their two souls will unite to-night in the effort to interpret the same idea by different means. There is no ground on which your soul and mine can meet. I love you. Too restless and sad to stay at home, I tramp here every day, six miles and back, to be met only by your indifference. I am poor, my family is large, you can have no inducement to marry a man who cannot even find sufficient food for his own mouth.

MASHA.   It is not that. [*She takes snuff*] I am touched by your affection, but I cannot return it, that is all. [*She offers him the snuff-box*] Will you take some?

MEDVIEDENKO.   No, thank you.

[*A pause.*

MASHA.   The air is sultry; a storm is brewing for to-night. You do nothing but moralise or else talk about money. To you, poverty is the greatest misfortune that can befall a man, but I think it is a thousand times easier to go begging in rags than to— You wouldn't understand that, though.

SORIN *leaning on a cane, and* TREPLIEFF *come in.*

SORIN.   For some reason, my boy, country life doesn't suit me, and I am sure I shall never get used to it. Last night I went to bed at ten and woke at nine this morning, feeling as if, from oversleep, my brain had stuck to my skull. [*Laughing*] And yet I accidentally dropped off to sleep again after dinner, and feel utterly done up at this moment. It is like a nightmare.

TREPLIEFF.   There is no doubt that you should live in town. [*He catches sight of* MASHA *and* MEDVIEDENKO] You shall be called when the play begins, my friends, but you must not stay here now. Go away, please.

SORIN.   Miss Masha, will you kindly ask your father to leave the dog unchained? It howled so last night that my sister was unable to sleep.

MASHA. You must speak to my father yourself. Please excuse me; I can't do so. [*To* MEDVIEDENKO] Come, let us go.

MEDVIEDENKO. You will let us know when the play begins?

MASHA *and* MEDVIEDENKO *go out.*

SORIN. I foresee that that dog is going to howl all night again. It is always this way in the country; I have never been able to live as I like here. I come down for a month's holiday, to rest and all, and am plagued so by their nonsense that I long to escape after the first day. [*Laughing*] I have always been glad to get away from this place, but I have been retired now, and this was the only place I had to come to. Willy-nilly, one must live somewhere.

JACOB. [*To* TREPLIEFF] We are going to take a swim, Mr. Constantine.

TREPLIEFF. Very well, but you must be back in ten minutes.

JACOB. We will, sir.

TREPLIEFF. [*Looking at the stage*] Just like a real theatre! See, there we have the curtain, the foreground, the background, and all. No artificial scenery is needed. The eye travels direct to the lake, and rests on the horizon. The curtain will be raised as the moon rises at half-past eight.

SORIN. Splendid!

TREPLIEFF. Of course the whole effect will be ruined if Nina is late. She should be here by now, but her father and stepmother watch her so closely that it is like stealing her from a prison to get her away from home. [*He straightens* SORIN's *collar*] Your hair and beard are all on end. Oughtn't you to have them trimmed?

SORIN. [*Smoothing his beard*] They are the tragedy of my existence. Even when I was young I always looked as if I were drunk, and all. Women have never liked me. [*Sitting down*] Why is my sister out of temper?

TREPLIEFF. Why? Because she is jealous and bored. [*Sitting down beside* SORIN] She is not acting this evening, but Nina is, and so she has set herself against me, and against the performance of the play, and against the play itself, which she hates without ever having read it.

SORIN. [*Laughing*] Does she, really?

TREPLIEFF. Yes, she is furious because Nina is going to have a success on this little stage. [*Looking at his watch*] My mother is a psychological curiosity. Without doubt brilliant and talented, capable of sobbing over a novel, of reciting all Nekrasoff's poetry by heart, and of nursing the sick like an angel of heaven, you should see what happens if any one begins praising Duse to her! She alone must be praised and written about, raved over, her marvellous acting in "La Dame aux Camélias" extolled to the skies. As she cannot get all that rubbish in the country, she grows peevish and cross, and thinks we are all against her, and to blame for it all. She is superstitious, too. She dreads burning three candles, and fears the thirteenth day of the month. Then she is stingy. I know for a fact that she has seventy thousand roubles in a bank at Odessa, but she is ready to burst into tears if you ask her to lend you a penny.

SORIN. You have taken it into your head that your mother dislikes your play, and the thought of it has excited you, and all. Keep calm; your mother adores you.

TREPLIEFF. [*Pulling a flower to pieces*] She loves me, loves me not; loves—loves me not; loves—loves me not! [*Laughing*] You see, she doesn't love me, and why should she? She likes life and love and gay clothes, and I am already twenty-five years old; a sufficient reminder to her that she is no longer young. When I am away she is only thirty-two, in my presence she is forty-three, and she hates me for it. She knows, too, that I despise the modern stage. She adores it, and imagines that she is working on it for the benefit of humanity and her sacred art, but to me the theatre is merely the vehicle of convention and prejudice. When the curtain rises on that little three-walled room, when those mighty geniuses, those high-priests of art, show us people in the act of eating, drinking, loving, walking, and wearing their coats, and attempt to extract a moral from their insipid talk; when playwrights give us under a thousand different guises the same, same, same old stuff, then I must needs run from it, as Maupassant ran from the Eiffel Tower that was about to crush him by its vulgarity.

SORIN. But we can't do without a theatre.

TREPLIEFF. No, but we must have it under a new form. If we can't do that, let us rather not have it at all. [*Looking at his watch*] I love my mother, I love her devotedly, but I think she leads a stupid life. She always has this man of letters of hers on her mind, and the newspapers are always frightening her to death, and I am tired of it. Plain, human egoism sometimes speaks in my heart, and I regret that my mother is a famous actress. If she were an ordinary woman I think I should be a happier man. What could be more intolerable and foolish than my position, Uncle, when I find myself the only nonentity among a crowd of her guests, all celebrated authors and artists? I feel that they only endure me because I am her son. Personally I am nothing, nobody. I pulled through my third year at college by the skin of my teeth, as they say. I have neither money nor brains, and on my passport you may read that I am simply a citizen of Kiev. So was my father, but he was a well-known actor. When the celebrities that frequent my mother's drawing-room deign to notice me at all, I know they only look at me to measure my insignificance; I read their thoughts, and suffer from humiliation.

SORIN. Tell me, by the way, what is Trigorin like? I can't understand him, he is always so silent.

TREPLIEFF. Trigorin is clever, simple, well-mannered, and a little, I might say, melancholic in disposition. Though still under forty, he is surfeited with praise. As for his stories, they are—how shall I put it?—pleasing, full of talent, but if you have read Tolstoi or Zola you somehow don't enjoy Trigorin.

SORIN. Do you know, my boy, I like literary men. I once passionately desired two things: to marry, and to become an author. I have succeeded in neither. It must be pleasant to be even an insignificant author.

TREPLIEFF. [Listening] I hear footsteps! [He embraces his uncle] I cannot live without her; even the sound of her footsteps is music to me. I am madly happy. [He goes quickly to meet NINA, who comes in at that moment] My enchantress! My girl of dreams!

NINA. [Excitedly] It can't be that I am late? No, I am not late.

TREPLIEFF. [Kissing her hands] No, no, no!

NINA. I have been in a fever all day, I was so afraid my father would prevent my coming, but he and my stepmother have just gone driving. The sky is clear, the moon is rising. How I hurried to get here! How I urged my horse to go faster and faster! [Laughing] I am so glad to see you!

[She shakes hands with SORIN.

SORIN.   Oho! Your eyes look as if you had been crying. You mustn't do that.

NINA.   It is nothing, nothing. Do let us hurry. I must go in half an hour. No, no, for heaven's sake do not urge me to stay. My father doesn't know I am here.

TREPLIEFF.   As a matter of fact, it is time to begin now. I must call the audience.

SORIN.   Let me call them—and all—I am going this minute. [*He goes toward the right, begins to sing "The Two Grenadiers," then stops.*] I was singing that once when a fellow-lawyer said to me: "You have a powerful voice, sir." Then he thought a moment and added, "But it is a disagreeable one!"

[*He goes out laughing.*

NINA.   My father and his wife never will let me come here; they call this place Bohemia and are afraid I shall become an actress. But this lake attracts me as it does the gulls. My heart is full of you.

[*She glances about her.*

TREPLIEFF.   We are alone.

NINA.   Isn't that some one over there?

TREPLIEFF.   No.

[*They kiss one another.*

NINA.   What is that tree?

TREPLIEFF.   An elm.

NINA.   Why does it look so dark?

TREPLIEFF.   It is evening; everything looks dark now. Don't go away early, I implore you.

NINA.   I must.

TREPLIEFF.   What if I were to follow you, Nina? I shall stand in your garden all night with my eyes on your window.

NINA.   That would be impossible; the watchman would see you, and Treasure is not used to you yet, and would bark.

TREPLIEFF.   I love you.

NINA.   Hush!

TREPLIEFF.   [*Listening to approaching footsteps*] Who is that? Is it you, Jacob?

JACOB.   [*On the stage*] Yes, sir.

TREPLIEFF.   To your places then. The moon is rising; the play must commence.

NINA. Yes, sir.

TREPLIEFF. Is the alcohol ready? Is the sulphur ready? There must be fumes of sulphur in the air when the red eyes shine out. [*To* NINA] Go, now, everything is ready. Are you nervous?

NINA. Yes, very. I am not so much afraid of your mother as I am of Trigorin. I am terrified and ashamed to act before him; he is so famous. Is he young?

TREPLIEFF. Yes.

NINA. What beautiful stories he writes!

TREPLIEFF. [*Coldly*] I have never read any of them, so I can't say.

NINA. Your play is very hard to act; there are no living characters in it.

TREPLIEFF. Living characters! Life must be represented not as it is, but as it ought to be; as it appears in dreams.

NINA. There is so little action; it seems more like a recitation. I think love should always come into every play.

> NINA *and* TREPLIEFF *go up onto the little stage;* PAULINA *and* DORN *come in.*

PAULINA. It is getting damp. Go back and put on your goloshes.

DORN. I am quite warm.

PAULINA. You never will take care of yourself; you are quite obstinate about it, and yet you are a doctor, and know quite well that damp air is bad for you. You like to see me suffer, that's what it is. You sat out on the terrace all yesterday evening on purpose.

DORN. [*Sings*]

> "Oh, tell me not that youth is wasted."

PAULINA. You were so enchanted by the conversation of Madame Arkadina that you did not even notice the cold. Confess that you admire her.

DORN. I am fifty-five years old.

PAULINA. A trifle. That is not old for a man. You have kept your looks magnificently, and women still like you.

DORN. What are you trying to tell me?

PAULINA.   You men are all ready to go down on your knees to an actress, all of you.

DORN.   [*Sings*]

"Once more I stand before thee."

It is only right that artists should be made much of by society and treated differently from, let us say, merchants. It is a kind of idealism.

PAULINA.   When women have loved you and thrown themselves at your head, has that been idealism?

DORN.   [*Shrugging his shoulders*] I can't say. There has been a great deal that was admirable in my relations with women. In me they liked, above all, the superior doctor. Ten years ago, you remember, I was the only decent doctor they had in this part of the country—and then, I have always acted like a man of honour.

PAULINA.   [*Seizes his hand*] Dearest!

DORN.   Be quiet! Here they come.

ARKADINA *comes in on* SORIN's *arm; also* TRIGORIN, SHAMRAEFF, MEDVIEDENKO, *and* MASHA.

SHAMRAEFF.   She acted most beautifully at the Poltava Fair in 1873; she was really magnificent. But tell me, too, where Tchadin the comedian is now? He was inimitable as Rasplueff, better than Sadofski. Where is he now?

ARKADINA.   Don't ask me where all those antediluvians are! I know nothing about them.

[*She sits down.*

SHAMRAEFF.   [*Sighing*] Pashka Tchadin! There are none left like him. The stage is not what it was in his time. There were sturdy oaks growing on it then, where now but stumps remain.

DORN.   It is true that we have few dazzling geniuses these days, but, on the other hand, the average of acting is much higher.

SHAMRAEFF.   I cannot agree with you; however, that is a matter of taste, *de gustibus*.

Enter TREPLIEFF *from behind the stage.*

ARKADINA.   When will the play begin, my dear boy?

TREPLIEFF.   In a moment. I must ask you to have patience.

ARKADINA.   [*Quoting from Hamlet*] My son,

"Thou turn'st mine eyes into my very soul;
And there I see such black grained spots
As will not leave their tinct."

[*A horn is blown behind the stage.*

TREPLIEFF.   Attention, ladies and gentlemen! The play is about to begin. [*A pause*] I shall commence. [*He taps the door with a stick, and speaks in a loud voice*] O, ye time-honoured, ancient mists that drive at night across the surface of this lake, blind you our eyes with sleep, and show us in our dreams that which will be in twice ten thousand years!

SORIN.   There won't be anything in twice ten thousand years.

TREPLIEFF.   Then let them now show us that nothingness.

ARKADINA.   Yes, let them—we are asleep.

The curtain rises. A vista opens across the lake. The moon hangs low above the horizon and is reflected in the water. NINA, dressed in white, is seen seated on a great rock.

NINA.   All men and beasts, lions, eagles, and quails, horned stags, geese, spiders, silent fish that inhabit the waves, starfish from the sea, and creatures invisible to the eye—in one word, life—all, all life, completing the dreary round imposed upon it, has died out at last. A thousand years have passed since the earth last bore a living creature on her breast, and the unhappy moon now lights her lamp in vain. No longer are the cries of storks heard in the meadows, or the drone of beetles in the groves of limes. All is cold, cold. All is void, void, void. All is terrible, terrible—[*A pause*] The bodies of all living creatures have dropped to dust, and eternal matter has transformed them into stones and water and clouds; but their spirits have flowed together into one, and that great world-soul am I! In me is the spirit of the great Alexander, the spirit of Napoleon, of Cæsar, of Shakespeare, and of the tiniest leech that swims. In me the consciousness of man has joined hands with the instinct of the animal; I understand all, all, all, and each life lives again in me.

[*The will-o-the-wisps flicker out along the lake shore.*
ARKADINA. [*Whispers*] What decadent rubbish is this?
TREPLIEFF. [*Imploringly*] Mother!
NINA. I am alone. Once in a hundred years my lips are opened, my voice echoes mournfully across the desert earth, and no one hears. And you, poor lights of the marsh, you do not hear me. You are engendered at sunset in the putrid mud, and flit wavering about the lake till dawn, unconscious, unreasoning, unwarmed by the breath of life. Satan, father of eternal matter, trembling lest the spark of life should glow in you, has ordered an unceasing movement of the atoms that compose you, and so you shift and change for ever. I, the spirit of the universe, I alone am immutable and eternal. [*A pause*] Like a captive in a dungeon deep and void, I know not where I am, nor what awaits me. One thing only is not hidden from me: in my fierce and obstinate battle with Satan, the source of the forces of matter, I am destined to be victorious in the end. Matter and spirit will then be one at last in glorious harmony, and the reign of freedom will begin on earth. But this can only come to pass by slow degrees, when after countless æons the moon and earth and shining Sirius himself shall fall to dust. Until that hour, oh, horror! horror! horror! [*A pause. Two glowing red points are seen shining across the lake*] Satan, my mighty foe, advances; I see his dread and lurid eyes.
ARKADINA. I smell sulphur. Is that done on purpose?
TREPLIEFF. Yes.
ARKADINA. Oh, I see; that is part of the effect.
TREPLIEFF. Mother!
NINA. He longs for man——
PAULINA. [*To* DORN] You have taken off your hat again! Put it on, you will catch cold.
ARKADINA. The doctor has taken off his hat to Satan, father of eternal matter——
TREPLIEFF. [*Loudly and angrily*] Enough of this! There's an end to the performance. Down with the curtain!
ARKADINA. Why, what are you so angry about?
TREPLIEFF. [*Stamping his foot*] The curtain; down with it! [*The curtain falls*] Excuse me, I forgot that only a chosen few

might write plays or act them. I have infringed the monopoly. I—
I—

> *He would like to say more, but waves his hand instead, and goes out to the left.*

ARKADINA. What is the matter with him?

SORIN. You should not handle youthful egoism so roughly, sister.

ARKADINA. What did I say to him?

SORIN. You hurt his feelings.

ARKADINA. But he told me himself that this was all in fun, so I treated his play as if it were a comedy.

SORIN. Nevertheless——

ARKADINA. Now it appears that he has produced a masterpiece, if you please! I suppose it was not meant to amuse us at all, but that he arranged the performance and fumigated us with sulphur to demonstrate to us how plays should be written, and what is worth acting. I am tired of him. No one could stand his constant thrusts and sallies. He is a wilful, egotistic boy.

SORIN. He had hoped to give you pleasure.

ARKADINA. Is that so? I notice, though, that he did not choose an ordinary play, but forced his decadent trash on us. I am willing to listen to any raving, so long as it is not meant seriously, but in showing us this, he pretended to be introducing us to a new form of art, and inaugurating a new era. In my opinion, there was nothing new about it, it was simply an exhibition of bad temper.

TRIGORIN. Everybody must write as he feels, and as best he may.

ARKADINA. Let him write as he feels and can, but let him spare me his nonsense.

DORN. Thou art angry, O Jove!

ARKADINA. I am a woman, not Jove. [*She lights a cigarette*] And I am not angry, I am only sorry to see a young man foolishly wasting his time. I did not mean to hurt him.

MEDVIEDENKO. No one has any ground for separating life from matter, as the spirit may well consist of the union of material atoms. [*Excitedly, to* TRIGORIN] Some day you should write a play, and put on the stage the life of a schoolmaster. It is a hard, hard life.

ARKADINA.   I agree with you, but do not let us talk about plays or atoms now. This is such a lovely evening. Listen to the singing, friends, how sweet it sounds.

PAULINA.   Yes, they are singing across the water.

[*A pause.*

ARKADINA.   [*To* TRIGORIN] Sit down beside me here. Ten or fifteen years ago we had music and singing on this lake almost all night. There are six houses on its shores. All was noise and laughter and romance then, such romance! The young star and idol of them all in those days was this man here, [*Nods toward* DORN] Doctor Eugene Dorn. He is fascinating now, but he was irresistible then. But my conscience is beginning to prick me. Why did I hurt my poor boy? I am uneasy about him. [*Loudly*] Constantine! Constantine!

MASHA.   Shall I go and find him?

ARKADINA.   If you please, my dear.

MASHA.   [*Goes off to the left, calling*] Mr. Constantine! Oh, Mr. Constantine!

NINA.   [*Comes in from behind the stage*] I see that the play will never be finished, so now I can go home. Good evening.

[*She kisses* ARKADINA *and* PAULINA.

SORIN.   Bravo! Bravo!

ARKADINA.   Bravo! Bravo! We were quite charmed by your acting. With your looks and such a lovely voice it is a crime for you to hide yourself in the country. You must be very talented. It is your duty to go on the stage, do you hear me?

NINA.   It is the dream of my life, which will never come true.

ARKADINA.   Who knows? Perhaps it will. But let me present Monsieur Boris Trigorin.

NINA.   I am delighted to meet you. [*Embarrassed*] I have read all your books.

ARKADINA.   [*Drawing* NINA *down beside her*] Don't be afraid of him, dear. He is a simple, good-natured soul, even if he is a celebrity. See, he is embarrassed himself.

DORN.   Couldn't the curtain be raised now? It is depressing to have it down.

SHAMRAEFF.   [*Loudly*] Jacob, my man! Raise the curtain!

NINA.   [*To* TRIGORIN] It was a curious play, wasn't it?

TRIGORIN.   Very. I couldn't understand it at all, but I watched it with the greatest pleasure because you acted with such sincerity, and the setting was beautiful. [*A pause*] There must be a lot of fish in this lake.

NINA.   Yes, there are.

TRIGORIN.   I love fishing. I know of nothing pleasanter than to sit on a lake shore in the evening with one's eyes on a floating cork.

NINA.   Why, I should think that for one who has tasted the joys of creation, no other pleasure could exist.

ARKADINA.   Don't talk like that. He always begins to flounder when people say nice things to him.

SHAMRAEFF.   I remember when the famous Silva was singing once in the Opera House at Moscow, how delighted we all were when he took the low C. Well, you can imagine our astonishment when one of the church cantors, who happened to be sitting in the gallery, suddenly boomed out: "Bravo, Silva!" a whole octave lower. Like this: [*In a deep bass voice*] "Bravo, Silva!" The audience was left breathless.

[*A pause.*

DORN.   An angel of silence is flying over our heads.

NINA.   I must go. Good-bye.

ARKADINA.   Where to? Where must you go so early? We shan't allow it.

NINA.   My father is waiting for me.

ARKADINA.   How cruel he is, really. [*They kiss each other*] Then I suppose we can't keep you, but it is very hard indeed to let you go.

NINA.   If you only knew how hard it is for me to leave you all.

ARKADINA.   Somebody must see you home, my pet.

NINA.   [*Startled*] No, no!

SORIN.   [*Imploringly*] Don't go!

NINA.   I must.

SORIN.   Stay just one hour more, and all. Come now, really, you know.

NINA.   [*Struggling against her desire to stay; through her tears*] No, no, I can't.

[*She shakes hands with him and quickly goes out.*

ARKADINA.   An unlucky girl! They say that her mother left the whole of an immense fortune to her husband, and now the child is penniless because the father has already willed everything away to his second wife. It is pitiful.

DORN.   Yes, her papa is a perfect beast, and I don't mind saying so—it is what he deserves.

SORIN.   [*Rubbing his chilled hands*] Come, let us go in; the night is damp, and my legs are aching.

ARKADINA.   Yes, you act as if they were turned to stone; you can hardly move them. Come, you unfortunate old man.

[*She takes his arm.*

SHAMRAEFF.   [*Offering his arm to his wife*] Permit me, madame.

SORIN.   I hear that dog howling again. Won't you please have it unchained, Shamraeff?

SHAMRAEFF.   No, I really can't, sir. The granary is full of millet, and I am afraid thieves might break in if the dog were not there. [*Walking beside* MEDVIEDENKO] Yes, a whole octave lower: "Bravo, Silva!" and he wasn't a singer either, just a simple church cantor.

MEDVIEDENKO.   What salary does the church pay its singers?

[*All go out except* DORN.

DORN.   I may have lost my judgment and my wits, but I must confess I liked that play. There was something in it. When the girl spoke of her solitude and the Devil's eyes gleamed across the lake, I felt my hands shaking with excitement. It was so fresh and naïve. But here he comes; let me say something pleasant to him.

TREPLIEFF *comes in.*

TREPLIEFF.   All gone already?

DORN.   I am here.

TREPLIEFF.   Masha has been yelling for me all over the park. An insufferable creature.

DORN.   Constantine, your play delighted me. It was strange, of course, and I did not hear the end, but it made a deep impression on me. You have a great deal of talent, and must persevere in your work.

TREPLIEFF *seizes his hand and squeezes it hard, then kisses him impetuously.*

DORN. Tut, tut! how excited you are. Your eyes are full of tears. Listen to me. You chose your subject in the realm of abstract thought, and you did quite right. A work of art should invariably embody some lofty idea. Only that which is seriously meant can ever be beautiful. How pale you are!

TREPLIEFF. So you advise me to persevere?

DORN. Yes, but use your talent to express only deep and eternal truths. I have led a quiet life, as you know, and am a contented man, but if I should ever experience the exaltation that an artist feels during his moments of creation, I think I should spurn this material envelope of my soul and everything connected with it, and should soar away into heights above this earth.

TREPLIEFF. I beg your pardon, but where is Nina?

DORN. And yet another thing: every work of art should have a definite object in view. You should know why you are writing, for if you follow the road of art without a goal before your eyes, you will lose yourself, and your genius will be your ruin.

TREPLIEFF. [Impetuously] Where is Nina?

DORN. She has gone home.

TREPLIEFF. [In despair] Gone home? What shall I do? I want to see her; I must see her! I shall follow her.

DORN. My dear boy, keep quiet.

TREPLIEFF. I am going. I must go.

MASHA comes in.

MASHA. Your mother wants you to come in, Mr. Constantine. She is waiting for you, and is very uneasy.

TREPLIEFF. Tell her I have gone away. And for heaven's sake, all of you, leave me alone! Go away! Don't follow me about!

DORN. Come, come, old chap, don't act like this; it isn't kind at all.

TREPLIEFF. [Through his tears] Good-bye, doctor, and thank you.

TREPLIEFF goes out.

DORN. [Sighing] Ah, youth, youth!

MASHA. It is always "Youth, youth," when there is nothing else to be said.

She takes snuff. DORN *takes the snuff-box out of her hands and flings it into the bushes.*

DORN.   Don't do that, it is horrid. [*A pause*] I hear music in the house. I must go in.

MASHA.   Wait a moment.

DORN.   What do you want?

MASHA.   Let me tell you again. I feel like talking. [*She grows more and more excited*] I do not love my father, but my heart turns to you. For some reason, I feel with all my soul that you are near to me. Help me! Help me, or I shall do something foolish and mock at my life, and ruin it. I am at the end of my strength.

DORN.   What is the matter? How can I help you?

MASHA.   I am in agony. No one, no one can imagine how I suffer. [*She lays her hand on his shoulder and speaks softly*] I love Constantine.

DORN.   Oh, how excitable you all are! And how much love there is about this lake of spells! [*Tenderly*] But what can I do for you, my child? What? What?

The curtain falls.

ACT II

The lawn in front of SORIN's *house. The house stands in the back-ground, on a broad terrace. The lake, brightly reflecting the rays of the sun, lies to the left. There are flower-beds here and there. It is noon; the day is hot.* ARKADINA, DORN, *and* MASHA *are sitting on a bench on the lawn, in the shade of an old linden. An open book is lying on* DORN's *knees.*

ARKADINA. [*To* MASHA] Come, get up. [*They both get up*] Stand beside me. You are twenty-two and I am almost twice your age. Tell me, Doctor, which of us is the younger looking?

DORN. You are, of course.

ARKADINA. You see! Now why is it? Because I work; my heart and mind are always busy, whereas you never move off the same spot. You don't live. It is a maxim of mine never to look into the future. I never admit the thought of old age or death, and just ac-cept what comes to me.

MASHA. I feel as if I had been in the world a thousand years, and I trail my life behind me like an endless scarf. Often I have no desire to live at all. Of course that is foolish. One ought to pull oneself together and shake off such nonsense.

DORN. [*Sings softly*]

"Tell her, oh flowers—"

ARKADINA. And then I keep myself as correct-looking as an Englishman. I am always well-groomed, as the saying is, and

17

carefully dressed, with my hair neatly arranged. Do you think I should ever permit myself to leave the house half-dressed, with untidy hair? Certainly not! I have kept my looks by never letting myself slump as some women do. [*She puts her arms akimbo, and walks up and down on the lawn*] See me, tripping on tiptoe like a fifteen-year-old girl.

DORN.   I see. Nevertheless, I shall continue my reading. [*He takes up his book*] Let me see, we had come to the grain-dealer and the rats.

ARKADINA.   And the rats. Go on. [*She sits down*] No, give me the book, it is my turn to read. [*She takes the book and looks for the place*] And the rats. Ah, here it is. [*She reads*] "It is as dangerous for society to attract and indulge authors as it is for grain-dealers to raise rats in their granaries. Yet society loves authors. And so, when a woman has found one whom she wishes to make her own, she lays siege to him by indulging and flattering him." That may be so in France, but it certainly is not so in Russia. We do not carry out a programme like that. With us, a woman is usually head over ears in love with an author before she attempts to lay siege to him. You have an example before your eyes, in me and Trigorin.

> SORIN *comes in leaning on a cane, with* NINA *beside him.*
> MEDVIEDENKO *follows, pushing an arm-chair.*

SORIN.   [*In a caressing voice, as if speaking to a child*] So we are happy now, eh? We are enjoying ourselves to-day, are we? Father and stepmother have gone away to Tver, and we are free for three whole days!

NINA.   [*Sits down beside* ARKADINA, *and embraces her*] I am so happy. I belong to you now.

SORIN.   [*Sits down in his arm-chair*] She looks lovely to-day.

ARKADINA.   Yes, she has put on her prettiest dress, and looks sweet. That was nice of you. [*She kisses* NINA] But we mustn't praise her too much; we shall spoil her. Where is Trigorin?

NINA.   He is fishing off the wharf.

ARKADINA.   I wonder he isn't bored.

> [*She begins to read again.*

NINA.   What are you reading?

ARKADINA.   "On the Water," by Maupassant. [*She reads a few lines to herself*] But the rest is neither true nor interesting. [*She lays down the book*] I am uneasy about my son. Tell me, what is the matter with him? Why is he so dull and depressed lately? He spends all his days on the lake, and I scarcely ever see him any more.

MASHA.   His heart is heavy. [*Timidly, to* NINA] Please recite something from his play.

NINA.   [*Shrugging her shoulders*] Shall I? Is it so interesting?

MASHA.   [*With suppressed rapture*] When he recites, his eyes shine and his face grows pale. His voice is beautiful and sad, and he has the ways of a poet.

SORIN *begins to snore.*

DORN.   Pleasant dreams!

ARKADINA.   Peter!

SORIN.   Eh?

ARKADINA.   Are you asleep?

SORIN.   Not a bit of it.

[*A pause.*

ARKADINA.   You don't do a thing for your health, brother, but you really ought to.

DORN.   The idea of doing anything for one's health at sixty-five!

SORIN.   One still wants to live at sixty-five.

DORN.   [*Crossly*] Ho! Take some camomile tea.

ARKADINA.   I think a journey to some watering-place would be good for him.

DORN.   Why, yes; he might go as well as not.

ARKADINA.   You don't understand.

DORN.   There is nothing to understand in this case; it is quite clear.

[*A pause.*

MEDVIEDENKO.   He ought to give up smoking.

SORIN.   What nonsense!

DORN.   No, that is not nonsense. Wine and tobacco destroy the individuality. After a cigar or a glass of vodka you are no longer Peter Sorin, but Peter Sorin plus somebody else. Your ego breaks in two: you begin to think of yourself in the third person.

SORIN.   It is easy for you to condemn smoking and drinking;

you have known what life is, but what about me? I have served in the Department of Justice for twenty-eight years, but I have never lived, I have never had any experiences. You are satiated with life, and that is why you have an inclination for philosophy, but I want to live, and that is why I drink my wine for dinner and smoke cigars, and all.

DORN. One must take life seriously, and to take a cure at sixty-five and regret that one did not have more pleasure in youth is, forgive my saying so, trifling.

MASHA. It must be lunch-time. [*She walks away languidly, with a dragging step*] My foot has gone to sleep.

DORN. She is going to have a couple of drinks before lunch.

SORIN. The poor soul is unhappy.

DORN. That is a trifle, your honour.

SORIN. You judge her like a man who has obtained all he wants in life.

ARKADINA. Oh, what could be duller than this dear tedium of the country? The air is hot and still, nobody does anything but sit and philosophise about life. It is pleasant, my friends, to sit and listen to you here, but I had rather a thousand times sit alone in the room of a hotel learning a role by heart.

NINA. [*With enthusiasm*] You are quite right. I understand how you feel.

SORIN. Of course it is pleasanter to live in town. One can sit in one's library with a telephone at one's elbow, no one comes in without being first announced by the footman, the streets are full of cabs, and all——

DORN. [*Sings*]

"Tell her, oh flowers—"

SHAMRAEFF *comes in, followed by* PAULINA.

SHAMRAEFF. Here they are. How do you do? [*He kisses* ARKADINA's *hand and then* NINA's] I am delighted to see you looking so well. [*To* ARKADINA] My wife tells me that you mean to go to town with her to-day. Is that so?

ARKADINA. Yes, that is what I had planned to do.

SHAMRAEFF. Hm—that is splendid, but how do you intend to

get there, madam? We are hauling rye to-day, and all the men are busy. What horses would you take?

ARKADINA.   What horses? How do I know what horses we shall have?

SORIN.   Why, we have the carriage horses.

SHAMRAEFF.   The carriage horses! And where am I to find the harness for them? This is astonishing! My dear madam, I have the greatest respect for your talents, and would gladly sacrifice ten years of my life for you, but I cannot let you have any horses to-day.

ARKADINA.   But if I must go to town? What an extraordinary state of affairs!

SHAMRAEFF.   You do not know, madam, what it is to run a farm.

ARKADINA.   [*In a burst of anger*] That is an old story! Under these circumstances I shall go back to Moscow this very day. Order a carriage for me from the village, or I shall go to the station on foot.

SHAMRAEFF.   [*Losing his temper*] Under these circumstances I resign my position. You must find yourself another manager.

[*He goes out.*

ARKADINA.   It is like this every summer: every summer I am insulted here. I shall never set foot here again.

She goes out to the left, in the direction of the wharf. In a few minutes she is seen entering the house, followed by TRIGORIN, *who carries a bucket and fishing-rod.*

SORIN.   [*Losing his temper*] What the deuce did he mean by his impudence? I want all the horses brought here at once!

NINA.   [*To* PAULINA] How could he refuse anything to Madame Arkadina, the famous actress? Is not every wish, every caprice even, of hers, more important than any farm work? This is incredible.

PAULINA.   [*In despair*] What can I do about it? Put yourself in my place and tell me what I can do.

SORIN.   [*To* NINA] Let us go and find my sister, and all beg her not to go. [*He looks in the direction in which* SHAMRAEFF *went out*] That man is insufferable; a regular tyrant.

NINA.   [*Preventing him from getting up*] Sit still, sit still, and let us wheel you. [*She and* MEDVIEDENKO *push the chair before them*] This is terrible!

SORIN.   Yes, yes, it is terrible; but he won't leave. I shall have a talk with him in a moment.

[*They go out. Only* DORN *and* PAULINA *are left.*

DORN.   How tiresome people are! Your husband deserves to be thrown out of here neck and crop, but it will all end by this old granny Sorin and his sister asking the man's pardon. See if it doesn't.

PAULINA.   He has sent the carriage horses into the fields too. These misunderstandings occur every day. If you only knew how they excite me! I am ill; see! I am trembling all over! I cannot endure his rough ways. [*Imploringly*] Eugene, my darling, my beloved, take me to you. Our time is short; we are no longer young; let us end deception and concealment, even though it is only at the end of our lives.

[*A pause.*

DORN.   I am fifty-five years old. It is too late now for me to change my ways of living.

PAULINA.   I know that you refuse me because there are other women who are near to you, and you cannot take everybody. I understand. Excuse me—I see I am only bothering you.

NINA *is seen near the house picking a bunch of flowers.*

DORN.   No, it is all right.

PAULINA.   I am tortured by jealousy. Of course you are a doctor and cannot escape from women. I understand.

DORN.   [*To* NINA, *who comes toward him*] How are things in there?

NINA.   Madame Arkadina is crying, and Sorin is having an attack of asthma.

DORN.   Let us go and give them both some camomile tea.

NINA.   [*Hands him the bunch of flowers*] Here are some flowers for you.

DORN.   Thank you.

[*He goes into the house.*

PAULINA.   [*Following him*] What pretty flowers! [*As they reach*

the house she says in a low voice] Give me those flowers! Give
them to me!

> Dorn *hands her the flowers; she tears them to pieces and
> flings them away. They both go into the house.*

Nina.   [*Alone*] How strange to see a famous actress weeping,
and for such a trifle! Is it not strange, too, that a famous author
should sit fishing all day? He is the idol of the public, the papers
are full of him, his photograph is for sale everywhere, his works
have been translated into many foreign languages, and yet he is
overjoyed if he catches a couple of minnows. I always thought famous people were distant and proud; I thought they despised the
common crowd which exalts riches and birth, and avenged
themselves on it by dazzling it with the inextinguishable honour
and glory of their fame. But here I see them weeping and playing cards and flying into passions like everybody else.

> Treplieff *comes in without a hat on, carrying a gun and a
> dead sea gull.*

Treplieff.   Are you alone here?
Nina.   Yes.

> Treplieff *lays the sea gull at her feet.*

Nina.   What do you mean by this?
Treplieff.   I was base enough to-day to kill this gull. I lay it
at your feet.
Nina.   What is happening to you?
>   [*She picks up the gull and stands looking at it.*
Treplieff.   [*After a pause*] So shall I soon end my own life.
Nina.   You have changed so that I fail to recognise you.
Treplieff.   Yes, I have changed since the time when I ceased
to recognise you. You have failed me; your look is cold; you do
not like to have me near you.
Nina.   You have grown so irritable lately, and you talk so
darkly and symbolically that you must forgive me if I fail to fol-
low you. I am too simple to understand you.
Treplieff.   All this began when my play failed so

dismally. A woman never can forgive failure. I have burnt the manuscript to the last page. Oh, if you could only fathom my unhappiness! Your estrangement is to me terrible, incredible; it is as if I had suddenly waked to find this lake dried up and sunk into the earth. You say you are too simple to understand me; but, oh, what is there to understand? You disliked my play, you have no faith in my powers, you already think of me as commonplace and worthless, as many are. [*Stamping his foot*] How well I can understand your feelings! And that understanding is to me like a dagger in the brain. May it be accursed, together with my stupidity, which sucks my life-blood like a snake! [*He sees* TRIGORIN, *who approaches reading a book*] There comes real genius, striding along like another Hamlet, and with a book, too. [*Mockingly*] "Words, words, words." You feel the warmth of that sun already, you smile, your eyes melt and glow liquid in its rays. I shall not disturb you.

[*He goes out.*

TRIGORIN. [*Making notes in his book*] Takes snuff and drinks vodka; always wears black dresses; is loved by a school-teacher——

NINA. How do you do?

TRIGORIN. How are you, Miss Nina? Owing to an unforeseen development of circumstances, it seems that we are leaving here to-day. You and I shall probably never see each other again, and I am sorry for it. I seldom meet a young and pretty girl now; I can hardly remember how it feels to be nineteen, and the young girls in my books are seldom living characters. I should like to change places with you, if but for an hour, to look out at the world through your eyes, and so find out what sort of a little person you are.

NINA. And I should like to change places with you.

TRIGORIN. Why?

NINA. To find out how a famous genius feels. What is it like to be famous? What sensations does it give you?

TRIGORIN. What sensations? I don't believe it gives any. [*Thoughtfully*] Either you exaggerate my fame, or else, if it exists, all I can say is that one simply doesn't feel fame in any way.

NINA. But when you read about yourself in the papers?

TRIGORIN.   If the critics praise me, I am happy; if they condemn me, I am out of sorts for the next two days.

NINA.   This is a wonderful world. If you only knew how I
envy you! Men are born to different destinies. Some dully drag a
weary, useless life behind them, lost in the crowd, unhappy,
while to one out of a million, as to you, for instance, comes a
bright destiny full of interest and meaning. You are lucky.

TRIGORIN.   I, lucky? [*He shrugs his shoulders*] H-m—I hear
you talking about fame, and happiness, and bright destinies, and
those fine words of yours mean as much to me—forgive my saying so—as sweetmeats do, which I never eat. You are very young,
and very kind.

NINA.   Your life is beautiful.

TRIGORIN.   I see nothing especially lovely about it. [*He looks
at his watch*] Excuse me, I must go at once, and begin writing
again. I am in a hurry. [*He laughs*] You have stepped on my pet
corn, as they say, and I am getting excited, and a little cross. Let
us discuss this bright and beautiful life of mine, though. [*After a
few moments' thought*] Violent obsessions sometimes lay hold of
a man: he may, for instance, think day and night of nothing but
the moon. I have such a moon. Day and night I am held in the
grip of one besetting thought, to write, write, write! Hardly have
I finished one book than something urges me to write another,
and then a third, and then a fourth—I write ceaselessly. I am, as
it were, on a treadmill. I hurry for ever from one story to another,
and can't help myself. Do you see anything bright and beautiful
in that? Oh, it is a wild life! Even now, thrilled as I am by talking
to you, I do not forget for an instant that an unfinished story is
awaiting me. My eye falls on that cloud there, which has the
shape of a grand piano; I instantly make a mental note that I
must remember to mention in my story a cloud floating by that
looked like a grand piano. I smell heliotrope; I mutter to myself:
a sickly smell, the colour worn by widows; I must remember that
in writing my next description of a summer evening. I catch an
idea in every sentence of yours or of my own, and hasten to lock
all these treasures in my literary store-room, thinking that some
day they may be useful to me. As soon as I stop working I rush off
to the theatre or go fishing, in the hope that I may find oblivion
there, but no! Some new subject for a story is sure to come

rolling through my brain like an iron cannonball. I hear my desk calling, and have to go back to it and begin to write, write, write, once more. And so it goes for everlasting. I cannot escape myself, though I feel that I am consuming my life. To prepare the honey I feed to unknown crowds, I am doomed to brush the bloom from my dearest flowers, to tear them from their stems, and trample the roots that bore them under foot. Am I not a madman? Should I not be treated by those who know me as one mentally diseased? Yet it is always the same, same old story, till I begin to think that all this praise and admiration must be a deception, that I am being hoodwinked because they know I am crazy, and I sometimes tremble lest I should be grabbed from behind and whisked off to a lunatic asylum. The best years of my youth were made one continual agony for me by my writing. A young author, especially if at first he does not make a success, feels clumsy, ill-at-ease, and superfluous in the world. His nerves are all on edge and stretched to the point of breaking; he is irresistibly attracted to literary and artistic people, and hovers about them unknown and unnoticed, fearing to look them bravely in the eye, like a man with a passion for gambling, whose money is all gone. I did not know my readers, but for some reason I imagined they were distrustful and unfriendly; I was mortally afraid of the public, and when my first play appeared, it seemed to me as if all the dark eyes in the audience were looking at it with enmity, and all the blue ones with cold indifference. Oh, how terrible it was! What agony!

NINA.   But don't your inspiration and the act of creation give you moments of lofty happiness?

TRIGORIN.   Yes. Writing is a pleasure to me, and so is reading the proofs, but no sooner does a book leave the press than it becomes odious to me; it is not what I meant it to be; I made a mistake to write it at all; I am provoked and discouraged. Then the public reads it and says: "Yes, it is clever and pretty, but not nearly as good as Tolstoi," or "It is a lovely thing, but not as good as Turgenieff's 'Fathers and Sons,'" and so it will always be. To my dying day I shall hear people say: "Clever and pretty, clever and pretty," and nothing more; and when I am gone, those that knew me will say as they pass my grave: "Here lies Trigorin, a clever writer, but he was not as good as Turgenieff."

NINA.   You must excuse me, but I decline to understand what you are talking about. The fact is, you have been spoilt by your success.

TRIGORIN.   What success have I had? I have never pleased myself; as a writer, I do not like myself at all. The trouble is that I am made giddy, as it were, by the fumes of my brain, and often hardly know what I am writing. I love this lake, these trees, the blue heaven; nature's voice speaks to me and wakes a feeling of passion in my heart, and I am overcome by an uncontrollable desire to write. But I am not only a painter of landscapes, I am a man of the city besides. I love my country, too, and her people; I feel that, as a writer, it is my duty to speak of their sorrows, of their future, also of science, of the rights of man, and so forth. So I write on every subject, and the public hounds me on all sides, sometimes in anger, and I race and dodge like a fox with a pack of hounds on his trail. I see life and knowledge flitting away before me. I am left behind them like a peasant who has missed his train at a station, and finally I come back to the conclusion that all I am fit for is to describe landscapes, and that whatever else I attempt rings abominably false.

NINA.   You work too hard to realise the importance of your writings. What if you are discontented with yourself? To others you appear a great and splendid man. If I were a writer like you I should devote my whole life to the service of the Russian people, knowing at the same time that their welfare depended on their power to rise to the heights I had attained, and the people should send me before them in a chariot of triumph.

TRIGORIN.   In a chariot? Do you think I am Agamemnon?
[*They both smile.*

NINA.   For the bliss of being a writer or an actress I could endure want, and disillusionment, and the hatred of my friends, and the pangs of my own dissatisfaction with myself; but I should demand in return fame, real, resounding fame! [*She covers her face with her hands*] Whew! My head reels!

THE VOICE OF ARKADINA.   [*From inside the house*] Boris! Boris!

TRIGORIN.   She is calling me, probably to come and pack, but I don't want to leave this place. [*His eyes rest on the lake*] What a blessing such beauty is!

NINA. Do you see that house there, on the far shore?

TRIGORIN. Yes.

NINA. That was my dead mother's home. I was born there, and have lived all my life beside this lake. I know every little island in it.

TRIGORIN. This is a beautiful place to live. [*He catches sight of the dead sea gull*] What is that?

NINA. A gull. Constantine shot it.

TRIGORIN. What a lovely bird! Really, I can't bear to go away. Can't you persuade Irina to stay?

[*He writes something in his note-book.*

NINA. What are you writing?

TRIGORIN. Nothing much, only an idea that occurred to me. [*He puts the book back in his pocket*] An idea for a short story. A young girl grows up on the shores of a lake, as you have. She loves the lake as the gulls do, and is as happy and free as they. But a man sees her who chances to come that way, and he destroys her out of idleness, as this gull here has been destroyed.

[*A pause.* ARKADINA *appears at one of the windows.*

ARKADINA. Boris! Where are you?

TRIGORIN. I am coming this minute.

He goes toward the house, looking back at NINA. ARKADINA *remains at the window.*

TRIGORIN. What do you want?

ARKADINA. We are not going away, after all.

TRIGORIN goes into the house. NINA comes forward and stands lost in thought.

NINA. It is a dream!

The curtain falls.

ACT III

The dining-room of SORIN's *house. Doors open out of it to the right and left. A table stands in the centre of the room. Trunks and boxes encumber the floor, and preparations for departure are evident.* TRIGORIN *is sitting at a table eating his breakfast, and* MASHA *is standing beside him.*

MASHA. I am telling you all these things because you write books and they may be useful to you. I tell you honestly, I should not have lived another day if he had wounded himself fatally. Yet I am courageous; I have decided to tear this love of mine out of my heart by the roots.

TRIGORIN. How will you do it?

MASHA. By marrying Medviedenko.

TRIGORIN. The school-teacher?

MASHA. Yes.

TRIGORIN. I don't see the necessity for that.

MASHA. Oh, if you knew what it is to love without hope for years and years, to wait for ever for something that will never come! I shall not marry for love, but marriage will at least be a change, and will bring new cares to deaden the memories of the past. Shall we have another drink?

TRIGORIN. Haven't you had enough?

MASHA. Fiddlesticks! [*She fills a glass*] Don't look at me with that expression on your face. Women drink oftener than you imagine, but most of them do it in secret, and not openly, as I do. They do indeed, and it is always either vodka or brandy. [*They*

29

touch glasses] To your good health! You are so easy to get on with that I am sorry to see you go.

[*They drink.*

TRIGORIN.   And I am sorry to leave.

MASHA.   You should ask her to stay.

TRIGORIN.   She would not do that now. Her son has been behaving outrageously. First he attempted suicide, and now I hear he is going to challenge me to a duel, though what his provocation may be I can't imagine. He is always sulking and sneering and preaching about a new form of art, as if the field of art were not large enough to accommodate both old and new without the necessity of jostling.

MASHA.   It is jealousy. However, that is none of my business. [*A pause.* JACOB *walks through the room carrying a trunk;* NINA *comes in and stands by the window*] That school-teacher of mine is none too clever, but he is very good, poor man, and he loves me dearly, and I am sorry for him. However, let me say good-bye and wish you a pleasant journey. Remember me kindly in your thoughts. [*She shakes hands with him*] Thanks for your goodwill. Send me your books, and be sure to write something in them; nothing formal, but simply this: "To Masha, who, forgetful of her origin, for some unknown reason is living in this world." Good-bye.

[*She goes out.*

NINA.   [*Holding out her closed hand to* TRIGORIN] Is it odd or even?

TRIGORIN.   Even.

NINA.   [*With a sigh*] No, it is odd. I had only one pea in my hand. I wanted to see whether I was to become an actress or not. If only some one would advise me what to do!

TRIGORIN.   One cannot give advice in a case like this.

[*A pause.*

NINA.   We shall soon part, perhaps never to meet again. I should like you to accept this little medallion as a remembrance of me. I have had your initials engraved on it, and on this side is the name of one of your books: "Days and Nights."

TRIGORIN.   How sweet of you! [*He kisses the medallion*] It is a lovely present.

NINA.   Think of me sometimes.

TRIGORIN.   I shall never forget you. I shall always remember you as I saw you that bright day—do you recall it?—a week ago, when you wore your light dress, and we talked together, and the white sea gull lay on the bench beside us.

NINA.   [*Lost in thought*] Yes, the sea gull. [*A pause*] I beg you to let me see you alone for two minutes before you go.

She goes out to the left. At the same moment ARKADINA *comes in from the right, followed by* SORIN *in a long coat, with his orders on his breast, and by* JACOB, *who is busy packing.*

ARKADINA.   Stay here at home, you poor old man. How could you pay visits with that rheumatism of yours? [*To* TRIGORIN] Who left the room just now, was it Nina?

TRIGORIN.   Yes.

ARKADINA.   I beg your pardon; I am afraid we interrupted you. [*She sits down*] I think everything is packed. I am absolutely exhausted.

TRIGORIN.   [*Reading the inscription on the medallion*] "Days and Nights, page 121, lines 11 and 12."

JACOB.   [*Clearing the table*] Shall I pack your fishing-rods, too, sir?

TRIGORIN.   Yes, I shall need them, but you can give my books away.

JACOB.   Very well, sir.

TRIGORIN.   [*To himself*] Page 121, lines 11 and 12. [*To* ARKADINA] Have we my books here in the house?

ARKADINA.   Yes, they are in my brother's library, in the corner cupboard.

TRIGORIN.   Page 121—

[*He goes out.*

SORIN.   You are going away, and I shall be lonely without you.

ARKADINA.   What would you do in town?

SORIN.   Oh, nothing in particular, but somehow—[*He laughs*] They are soon to lay the corner-stone of the new court-house here. How I should like to leap out of this minnow-pond, if but for an hour or two! I am tired of lying here like an old cigarette stump. I have ordered the carriage for one o'clock. We can go away together.

ARKADINA. [*After a pause*] No, you must stay here. Don't be lonely, and don't catch cold. Keep an eye on my boy. Take good care of him; guide him along the proper paths. [*A pause*] I am going away, and so shall never find out why Constantine shot himself, but I think the chief reason was jealousy, and the sooner I take Trigorin away, the better.

SORIN. There were—how shall I explain it to you?—other reasons besides jealousy for his act. Here is a clever young chap living in the depths of the country, without money or position, with no future ahead of him, and with nothing to do. He is ashamed and afraid of being so idle. I am devoted to him and he is fond of me, but nevertheless he feels that he is useless here, that he is little more than a dependent in this house. It is the pride in him.

ARKADINA. He is a misery to me! [*Thoughtfully*] He might possibly enter the army.

SORIN. [*Gives a whistle, and then speaks with hesitation*] It seems to me that the best thing for him would be if you were to let him have a little money. For one thing, he ought to be allowed to dress like a human being. See how he looks! Wearing the same little old coat that he has had for three years, and he doesn't even possess an overcoat! [*Laughing*] And it wouldn't hurt the youngster to sow a few wild oats; let him go abroad, say, for a time. It wouldn't cost much.

ARKADINA. Yes, but— However, I think I might manage about his clothes, but I couldn't let him go abroad. And no, I don't think I can let him have his clothes even, now. [*Decidedly*] I have no money at present.

SORIN *laughs.*

ARKADINA. I haven't indeed.

SORIN. [*Whistles*] Very well. Forgive me, darling; don't be angry. You are a noble, generous woman!

ARKADINA. [*Weeping*] I really haven't the money.

SORIN. If I had any money of course I should let him have some myself, but I haven't even a penny. The farm manager takes my pension from me and puts it all into the farm or into cattle or bees, and in that way it is always lost for ever. The bees die, the cows die, they never let me have a horse.

ARKADINA. Of course I have some money, but I am an actress and my expenses for dress alone are enough to bankrupt me.

SORIN. You are a dear, and I am very fond of you, indeed I am. But something is the matter with me again. [*He staggers*] I feel giddy. [*He leans against the table*] I feel faint, and all.

ARKADINA. [*Frightened*] Peter! [*She tries to support him*] Peter! dearest! [*She calls*] Help! Help!

TREPLIEFF *and* MEDVIEDENKO *come in;* TREPLIEFF *has a bandage around his head.*

ARKADINA. He is fainting!

SORIN. I am all right. [*He smiles and drinks some water*] It is all over now.

TREPLIEFF. [*To his mother*] Don't be frightened, mother, these attacks are not dangerous; my uncle often has them now. [*To his uncle*] You must go and lie down, Uncle.

SORIN. Yes, I think I shall, for a few minutes. I am going to Moscow all the same, but I shall lie down a bit before I start.

[*He goes out leaning on his cane.*

MEDVIEDENKO. [*Giving him his arm*] Do you know this riddle? On four legs in the morning; on two legs at noon; and on three legs in the evening?

SORIN. [*Laughing*] Yes, exactly, and on one's back at night. Thank you, I can walk alone.

MEDVIEDENKO. Dear me, what formality!

[*He and* SORIN *go out.*

ARKADINA. He gave me a dreadful fright.

TREPLIEFF. It is not good for him to live in the country. Mother, if you would only untie your purse-strings for once, and lend him a thousand roubles! He could then spend a whole year in town.

ARKADINA. I have no money. I am an actress and not a banker.

[*A pause.*

TREPLIEFF. Please change my bandage for me, mother, you do it so gently.

ARKADINA *goes to the cupboard and takes out a box of bandages and a bottle of iodoform.*

ARKADINA.   The doctor is late.

TREPLIEFF.   Yes, he promised to be here at nine, and now it is noon already.

ARKADINA.   Sit down. [*She takes the bandage off his head*] You look as if you had a turban on. A stranger that was in the kitchen yesterday asked to what nationality you belonged. Your wound is almost healed. [*She kisses his head*] You won't be up to any more of these silly tricks again, will you, when I am gone?

TREPLIEFF.   No, mother. I did that in a moment of insane despair, when I had lost all control over myself. It will never happen again. [*He kisses her hand*] Your touch is golden. I remember when you were still acting at the State Theatre, long ago, when I was still a little chap, there was a fight one day in our court, and a poor washerwoman was almost beaten to death. She was picked up unconscious, and you nursed her till she was well, and bathed her children in the washtubs. Have you forgotten it?

ARKADINA.   Yes, entirely.

[*She puts on a new bandage.*

TREPLIEFF.   Two ballet dancers lived in the same house, and they used to come and drink coffee with you.

ARKADINA.   I remember that.

TREPLIEFF.   They were very pious. [*A pause*] I love you again, these last few days, as tenderly and trustingly as I did as a child. I have no one left me now but you. Why, why do you let yourself be controlled by that man?

ARKADINA.   You don't understand him, Constantine. He has a wonderfully noble personality.

TREPLIEFF.   Nevertheless, when he has been told that I wish to challenge him to a duel his nobility does not prevent him from playing the coward. He is about to beat an ignominious retreat.

ARKADINA.   What nonsense! I have asked him myself to go.

TREPLIEFF.   A noble personality indeed! Here we are almost quarrelling over him, and he is probably in the garden laughing at us at this very moment, or else enlightening Nina's mind and trying to persuade her into thinking him a man of genius.

ARKADINA.   You enjoy saying unpleasant things to me. I have the greatest respect for that man, and I must ask you not to speak ill of him in my presence.

TREPLIEFF.   I have no respect for him at all. You want me to think him a genius, as you do, but I refuse to lie: his books make me sick.

ARKADINA.   You envy him. There is nothing left for people with no talent and mighty pretensions to do but to criticise those who are really gifted. I hope you enjoy the consolation it brings.

TREPLIEFF.   [*With irony*] Those who are really gifted, indeed! [*Angrily*] I am cleverer than any of you, if it comes to that! [*He tears the bandage off his head*] You are the slaves of convention, you have seized the upper hand and now lay down as law everything that you do; all else you strangle and trample on. I refuse to accept your point of view, yours and his, I refuse!

ARKADINA.   That is the talk of a decadent.

TREPLIEFF.   Go back to your beloved stage and act the miserable ditch-water plays you so much admire!

ARKADINA.   I never acted in a play like that in my life. You couldn't write even the trashiest music-hall farce, you idle good-for-nothing!

TREPLIEFF.   Miser!

ARKADINA.   Rag-bag!

TREPLIEFF *sits down and begins to cry softly.*

ARKADINA.   [*Walking up and down in great excitement*] Don't cry! You mustn't cry! [*She bursts into tears*] You really mustn't. [*She kisses his forehead, his cheeks, his head*] My darling child, forgive me. Forgive your wicked mother.

TREPLIEFF.   [*Embracing her*] Oh, if you could only know what it is to have lost everything under heaven! She does not love me. I see I shall never be able to write. Every hope has deserted me.

ARKADINA.   Don't despair. This will all pass. He is going away to-day, and she will love you once more. [*She wipes away his tears*] Stop crying. We have made peace again.

TREPLIEFF.   [*Kissing her hand*] Yes, mother.

ARKADINA.   [*Tenderly*] Make your peace with him, too. Don't fight with him. You surely won't fight?

TREPLIEFF.   I won't, but you must not insist on my seeing him again, mother, I couldn't stand it. [TRIGORIN *comes in*] There he is; I am going. [*He quickly puts the medicines away in the cupboard*] The doctor will attend to my head.

TREGORIN.   [*Looking through the pages of a book*] Page 121, lines 11 and 12; here it is. [*He reads*] "If at any time you should have need of my life, come and take it."

TREPLIEFF *picks up the bandage off the floor and goes out.*

ARKADINA.   [*Looking at her watch*] The carriage will soon be here.

TRIGORIN.   [*To himself*] If at any time you should have need of my life, come and take it.

ARKADINA.   I hope your things are all packed.

TRIGORIN.   [*Impatiently*] Yes, yes. [*In deep thought*] Why do I hear a note of sadness that wrings my heart in this cry of a pure soul? If at any time you should have need of my life, come and take it. [*To* ARKADINA] Let us stay here one more day!

ARKADINA *shakes her head*

TRIGORIN.   Do let us stay!

ARKADINA.   I know, dearest, what keeps you here, but you must control yourself. Be sober; your emotions have intoxicated you a little.

TRIGORIN.   You must be sober, too. Be sensible; look upon what has happened as a true friend would. [*Taking her hand*] You are capable of self-sacrifice. Be a friend to me and release me!

ARKADINA.   [*In deep excitement*] Are you so much in love?

TRIGORIN.   I am irresistibly impelled toward her. It may be that this is just what I need.

ARKADINA.   What, the love of a country girl? Oh, how little you know yourself!

TRIGORIN.   People sometimes walk in their sleep, and so I feel as if I were asleep, and dreaming of her as I stand here talking to you. My imagination is shaken by the sweetest and most glorious visions. Release me!

ARKADINA.   [*Shuddering*] No, no! I am only an ordinary woman; you must not say such things to me. Do not torment me, Boris; you frighten me.

TRIGORIN.   You could be an extraordinary woman if you only would. Love alone can bring happiness on earth, love the enchanting, the poetical love of youth, that sweeps away the sorrows of the world. I had no time for it when I was young and struggling with want and laying siege to the literary fortress, but now at last this love has come to me. I see it beckoning; why should I fly?

ARKADINA.   [*With anger*] You are mad!

TRIGORIN.   Release me.

ARKADINA.   You have all conspired together to torture me to-day.

[*She weeps.*

TRIGORIN.   [*Clutching his head desperately*] She doesn't understand me! She won't understand me!

ARKADINA.   Am I then so old and ugly already that you can talk to me like this without any shame about another woman? [*She embraces and kisses him*] Oh, you have lost your senses! My splendid, my glorious friend, my love for you is the last chapter of my life. [*She falls on her knees*] You are my pride, my joy, my light. [*She embraces his knees*] I could never endure it should you desert me, if only for an hour; I should go mad. Oh, my wonder, my marvel, my king!

TRIGORIN.   Some one might come in.

[*He helps her to rise.*

ARKADINA.   Let them come! I am not ashamed of my love. [*She kisses his hands*] My jewel! My despair! You want to do a foolish thing, but I don't want you to do it. I shan't let you do it! [*She laughs*] You are mine, you are mine! This forehead is mine, these eyes are mine, this silky hair is mine. All your being is mine. You are so clever, so wise, the first of all living writers; you are the only hope of your country. You are so fresh, so simple, so deeply humourous. You can bring out every feature of a man or of a landscape in a single line, and your characters live and breathe. Do you think that these words are but the incense of flattery? Do you think I am not speaking the truth? Come, look into my eyes; look deep; do you find lies there? No, you see that I alone know how to treasure you. I alone tell you the truth. Oh, my very dear, you will go with me? You will? You will not forsake me?

TRIGORIN.   I have no will of my own; I never had. I am too indolent, too submissive, too phlegmatic, to have any. Is it possible that women like that? Take me. Take me away with you, but do not let me stir a step from your side.

ARKADINA.   [*To herself*] Now he is mine! [*Carelessly, as if nothing unusual had happened*] Of course you must stay here if you really want to. I shall go, and you can follow in a week's time. Yes, really, why should you hurry away?

TRIGORIN.   Let us go together.

ARKADINA.   As you like. Let us go together then. [*A pause.* TRIGORIN *writes something in his note-book*] What are you writing?

TRIGORIN.   A happy expression I heard this morning: "A grove of maiden pines." It may be useful. [*He yawns*] So we are really off again, condemned once more to railway carriages, to stations and restaurants, to Hamburger steaks and endless arguments!

SHAMRAEFF *comes in.*

SHAMRAEFF.   I am sorry to have to inform you that your carriage is at the door. It is time to start, honoured madam, the train leaves at two-five. Would you be kind enough, madam, to remember to inquire for me where Suzdaltzeff the actor is now? Is he still alive, I wonder? Is he well? He and I have had many a jolly time together. He was inimitable in "The Stolen Mail." A tragedian called Izmailoff was in the same company, I remember, who was also quite remarkable. Don't hurry, madam, you still have five minutes. They were both of them conspirators once, in the same melodrama, and one night when in the course of the play they were suddenly discovered, instead of saying "We have been trapped!" Izmailoff cried out: "We have been rapped!" [*He laughs*] Rapped!

While he has been talking JACOB *has been busy with the trunks, and the maid has brought* ARKADINA *her hat, coat, parasol, and gloves. The cook looks hesitatingly through the door on the right, and finally comes into the room.* PAULINA *comes in.* MEDVIEDENKO *comes in.*

PAULINA.   [*Presenting* ARKADINA *with a little basket*] Here are some plums for the journey. They are very sweet ones. You may want to nibble something good on the way.

ARKADINA.   You are very kind, Paulina.

PAULINA.   Good-bye, my dearie. If things have not been quite as you could have wished, please forgive us.

[*She weeps.*

ARKADINA.   It has been delightful, delightful. You mustn't cry.

SORIN *comes in through the door on the left, dressed in a long coat with a cape, and carrying his hat and cane. He crosses the room.*

SORIN.   Come, sister, it is time to start, unless you want to miss the train. I am going to get into the carriage.

[*He goes out.*

MEDVIEDENKO.   I shall walk quickly to the station and see you off there.

[*He goes out.*

ARKADINA.   Good-bye, all! We shall meet again next summer if we live. [*The maid servant,* JACOB, *and the cook kiss her hand*] Don't forget me. [*She gives the cook a rouble*] There is a rouble for all three of you.

THE COOK.   Thank you, mistress; a pleasant journey to you.

JACOB.   God bless you, mistress.

SHAMRAEFF.   Send us a line to cheer us up. [*To* TRIGORIN] Good-bye, sir.

ARKADINA.   Where is Constantine? Tell him I am starting. I must say good-bye to him. [*To* JACOB] I gave the cook a rouble for all three of you.

All go out through the door on the right. The stage remains empty. Sounds of farewell are heard. The maid comes running back to fetch the basket of plums which has been forgotten. TRIGORIN *comes back.*

TRIGORIN.   I had forgotten my cane. I think I left it on the terrace. [*He goes toward the door on the right and meets* NINA, *who comes in at that moment*] Is that you? We are off.

NINA.   I knew we should meet again. [*With emotion*] I have come to an irrevocable decision, the die is cast: I am going on the stage. I am deserting my father and abandoning everything. I am beginning life anew. I am going, as you are, to Moscow. We shall meet there.

TRIGORIN.   [*Glancing about him*] Go to the Hotel Slavianski

Bazar. Let me know as soon as you get there. I shall be at the Grosholski House in Moltchanofka Street. I must go now.

[*A pause.*

NINA.   Just one more minute!

TRIGORIN.   [*In a low voice*] You are so beautiful! What bliss to think that I shall see you again so soon! [*She sinks on his breast*] I shall see those glorious eyes again, that wonderful, ineffably tender smile, those gentle features with their expression of angelic purity! My darling!

[*A prolonged kiss.*

The curtain falls.

Two years elapse between the third and fourth acts.

ACT IV

A sitting-room in SORIN's *house, which has been converted into a writing-room for* TREPLIEFF. *To the right and left are doors leading into inner rooms, and in the centre is a glass door opening onto a terrace. Besides the usual furniture of a sitting-room there is a writing-desk in the right-hand corner of the room. There is a Turkish divan near the door on the left, and shelves full of books stand against the walls. Books are lying scattered about on the window-sills and chairs. It is evening. The room is dimly lighted by a shaded lamp on a table. The wind moans in the tree tops and whistles down the chimney. The watchman in the garden is heard sounding his rattle.* MEDVIEDENKO *and* MASHA *come in.*

MASHA.   [*Calling* TREPLIEFF] Mr. Constantine, where are you? [*Looking about her*] There is no one here. His old uncle is forever asking for Constantine, and can't live without him for an instant.

MEDVIEDENKO.   He dreads being left alone. [*Listening to the wind*] This is a wild night. We have had this storm for two days.

MASHA.   [*Turning up the lamp*] The waves on the lake are enormous.

MEDVIEDENKO.   It is very dark in the garden. Do you know, I think that old theatre ought to be knocked down. It is still standing there, naked and hideous as a skeleton, with the curtain flapping in the wind. I thought I heard a voice weeping in it as I passed there last night.

MASHA.   What an idea!

[*A pause.*

MEDVIEDENKO.   Come home with me, Masha.

MASHA.   [*Shaking her head*] I shall spend the night here.

MEDVIEDENKO.   [*Imploringly*] Do come, Masha. The baby
must be hungry.

MASHA.   Nonsense, Matriona will feed it.

[*A pause.*

MEDVIEDENKO.   It is a pity to leave him three nights without
his mother.

MASHA.   You are getting too tiresome. You used sometimes to
talk of other things besides home and the baby, home and the
baby. That is all I ever hear from you now.

MEDVIEDENKO.   Come home, Masha.

MASHA.   You can go home if you want to.

MEDVIEDENKO.   Your father won't give me a horse.

MASHA.   Yes, he will; ask him.

MEDVIEDENKO.   I think I shall. Are you coming home
to-morrow?

MASHA.   Yes, yes, to-morrow.

She takes snuff. TREPLIEFF *and* PAULINA *come in.* TREPLIEFF
is carrying some pillows and a blanket, and PAULINA *is carrying sheets and pillow cases. They lay them on the divan,
and* TREPLIEFF *goes and sits down at his desk.*

MASHA.   Who is that for, mother?

PAULINA.   Mr. Sorin asked to sleep in Constantine's room
to-night.

MASHA.   Let me make the bed.

She makes the bed. PAULINA *goes up to the desk and looks at
the manuscripts lying on it. A pause.*

MEDVIEDENKO.   Well, I am going. Good-bye, Masha. [*He
kisses his wife's hand*] Good-bye, mother.

[*He tries to kiss his mother-in-law's hand.*

PAULINA.   [*Crossly*] Be off, in God's name!

TREPLIEFF *shakes hands with him in silence, and*
MEDVIEDENKO *goes out.*

PAULINA. [*Looking at the manuscripts*] No one ever dreamed, Constantine, that you would one day turn into a real author. The magazines pay you well for your stories. [*She strokes his hair.*] You have grown handsome, too. Dear, kind Constantine, be a little nicer to my Masha.

MASHA. [*Still making the bed*] Leave him alone, mother.

PAULINA. She is a sweet child. [*A pause*] A woman, Constantine, asks only for kind looks. I know that from experience.

TREPLIEFF *gets up from his desk and goes out without a word.*

MASHA. There now! You have vexed him. I told you not to bother him.

PAULINA. I am sorry for you, Masha.

MASHA. Much I need your pity!

PAULINA. My heart aches for you. I see how things are, and understand.

MASHA. You see what doesn't exist. Hopeless love is only found in novels. It is a trifle; all one has to do is to keep a tight rein on oneself, and keep one's head clear. Love must be plucked out the moment it springs up in the heart. My husband has been promised a school in another district, and when we have once left this place I shall forget it all. I shall tear my passion out by the roots.

[*The notes of a melancholy waltz are heard in the distance.*

PAULINA. Constantine is playing. That means he is sad.

MASHA *silently waltzes a few turns to the music.*

MASHA. The great thing, mother, is not to have him continually in sight. If my Simon could only get his remove I should forget it all in a month or two. It is a trifle.

DORN *and* MEDVIEDENKO *come in through the door on the left, wheeling* SORIN *in an arm-chair.*

MEDVIEDENKO. I have six mouths to feed now, and flour is at seventy kopecks.

DORN. A hard riddle to solve!

MEDVIEDENKO.   It is easy for you to make light of it. You are rich enough to scatter money to your chickens, if you wanted to.

DORN.   You think I am rich? My friend, after practising for thirty years, during which I could not call my soul my own for one minute of the night or day, I succeeded at last in scraping together one thousand roubles, all of which went, not long ago, in a trip which I took abroad. I haven't a penny.

MASHA.   [*To her husband*] So you didn't go home after all?

MEDVIEDENKO.   [*Apologetically*] How can I go home when they won't give me a horse?

MASHA.   [*Under her breath, with bitter anger*] Would I might never see your face again!

SORIN *in his chair is wheeled to the left-hand side of the room. * PAULINA, MASHA, *and* DORN *sit down beside him. * MEDVIEDENKO *stands sadly aside.*

DORN.   What a lot of changes you have made here! You have turned this sitting-room into a library.

MASHA.   Constantine likes to work in this room, because from it he can step out into the garden to meditate whenever he feels like it.

[*The watchman's rattle is heard.*

SORIN.   Where is my sister?

DORN.   She has gone to the station to meet Trigorin. She will soon be back.

SORIN.   I must be dangerously ill if you had to send for my sister. [*He falls silent for a moment*] A nice business this is! Here I am dangerously ill, and you won't even give me any medicine.

DORN.   What shall I prescribe for you? Camomile tea? Soda? Quinine?

SORIN.   Don't inflict any of your discussions on me again. [*He nods toward the sofa*] Is that bed for me?

PAULINA.   Yes, for you, sir.

SORIN.   Thank you.

DORN.   [*Sings*] "The moon swims in the sky to-night."

SORIN.   I am going to give Constantine an idea for a story. It shall be called "The Man Who Wished—*L'Homme qui a voulu.*" When I was young, I wished to become an author; I failed. I wished to be an orator; I speak abominably, [*Exciting himself*]

with my eternal "and all, and all," dragging each sentence on and
on until I sometimes break out into a sweat all over. I wished to
marry, and I didn't; I wished to live in the city, and here I am end-
ing my days in the country, and all.

DORN.   You wished to become State Councillor, and—you
are one!

SORIN.   [*Laughing*] I didn't try for that, it came of its own
accord.

DORN.   Come, you must admit that it is petty to cavil at life
at sixty-two years of age.

SORIN.   You are pig-headed! Can't you see I want to live?

DORN.   That is futile. Nature has commanded that every life
shall come to an end.

SORIN.   You speak like a man who is satiated with life. Your
thirst for it is quenched, and so you are calm and indifferent, but
even you dread death.

DORN.   The fear of death is an animal passion which must be
overcome. Only those who believe in a future life and tremble
for sins committed, can logically fear death; but you, for one
thing, don't believe in a future life, and for another, you haven't
committed any sins. You have served as a Councillor for twenty-
five years, that is all.

SORIN.   [*Laughing*] Twenty-eight years!

> TREPLIEFF *comes in and sits down on a stool at* SORIN's *feet.*
> MASHA *fixes her eyes on his face and never once tears them
> away.*

DORN.   We are keeping Constantine from his work.

TREPLIEFF.   No matter.

[*A pause.*

MEDVIEDENKO.   Of all the cities you visited when you were
abroad, Doctor, which one did you like the best?

DORN.   Genoa.

TREPLIEFF.   Why Genoa?

DORN.   Because there is such a splendid crowd in its streets.
When you leave the hotel in the evening, and throw yourself into
the heart of that throng, and move with it without aim or object,
swept along, hither and thither, their life seems to be yours, their
soul flows into you, and you begin to believe at last in a great

world spirit, like the one in your play that Nina Zarietchnaya acted. By the way, where is Nina now? Is she well?

TREPLIEFF.   I believe so.

DORN.   I hear she has led rather a strange life; what happened?

TREPLIEFF.   It is a long story, Doctor.

DORN.   Tell it shortly.

[A *pause.*

TREPLIEFF.   She ran away from home and joined Trigorin; you know that?

DORN.   Yes.

TREPLIEFF.   She had a child that died. Trigorin soon tired of her and returned to his former ties, as might have been expected. He had never broken them, indeed, but out of weakness of character had always vacillated between the two. As far as I can make out from what I have heard, Nina's domestic life has not been altogether a success.

DORN.   What about her acting?

TREPLIEFF.   I believe she made an even worse failure of that. She made her debut on the stage of the Summer Theatre in Moscow, and afterward made a tour of the country towns. At that time I never let her out of my sight, and wherever she went I followed. She always attempted great and difficult parts, but her delivery was harsh and monotonous, and her gestures heavy and crude. She shrieked and died well at times, but those were but moments.

DORN.   Then she really has a talent for acting?

TREPLIEFF.   I never could make out. I believe she has. I saw her, but she refused to see me, and her servant would never admit me to her rooms. I appreciated her feelings, and did not insist upon a meeting. [A *pause*] What more can I tell you? She sometimes writes to me now that I have come home, such clever, sympathetic letters, full of warm feeling. She never complains, but I can tell that she is profoundly unhappy; not a line but speaks to me of an aching, breaking nerve. She has one strange fancy; she always signs herself "The Sea Gull." The miller in "Rusalka" called himself "The Crow," and so she repeats in all her letters that she is a sea gull. She is here now.

DORN.   What do you mean by "here?"

TREPLIEFF.   In the village, at the inn. She has been there for five days. I should have gone to see her, but Masha here went, and she refuses to see any one. Some one told me she had been seen wandering in the fields a mile from here yesterday evening.

MEDVIEDENKO.   Yes, I saw her. She was walking away from here in the direction of the village. I asked her why she had not been to see us. She said she would come.

TREPLIEFF.   But she won't. [*A pause*] Her father and step-mother have disowned her. They have even put watchmen all around their estate to keep her away. [*He goes with the doctor toward the desk*] How easy it is, Doctor, to be a philosopher on paper, and how difficult in real life!

SORIN.   She was a beautiful girl. Even the State Councillor himself was in love with her for a time.

DORN.   You old Lovelace, you!

SHAMRAEFF's *laugh is heard.*

PAULINA.   They are coming back from the station.

TREPLIEFF.   Yes, I hear my mother's voice.

ARKADINA *and* TRIGORIN *come in, followed by* SHAMRAEFF.

SHAMRAEFF.   We all grow old and wither, my lady, while you alone, with your light dress, your gay spirits, and your grace, keep the secret of eternal youth.

ARKADINA.   You are still trying to turn my head, you tiresome old man.

TRIGORIN.   [*To* SORIN] How do you do, Peter? What, still ill? How silly of you! [*With evident pleasure, as he catches sight of* MASHA] How are you, Miss Masha?

MASHA.   So you recognised me?

[*She shakes hands with him.*

TRIGORIN.   Did you marry him?

MASHA.   Long ago.

TRIGORIN.   You are happy now? [*He bows to* DORN *and* MEDVIEDENKO, *and then goes hesitatingly toward* TREPLIEFF] Your mother says you have forgotten the past and are no longer angry with me.

TREPLIEFF *gives him his hand.*

ARKADINA. [*To her son*] Here is a magazine that Boris has brought you with your latest story in it.

TREPLIEFF. [*To* TRIGORIN, *as he takes the magazine*] Many thanks; you are very kind.

TRIGORIN. Your admirers all send you their regards. Every one in Moscow and St. Petersburg is interested in you, and all ply me with questions about you. They ask me what you look like, how old you are, whether you are fair or dark. For some reason they all think that you are no longer young, and no one knows who you are, as you always write under an assumed name. You are as great a mystery as the Man in the Iron Mask.

TREPLIEFF. Do you expect to be here long?

TRIGORIN. No, I must go back to Moscow to-morrow. I am finishing another novel, and have promised something to a magazine besides. In fact, it is the same old business.

During their conversation ARKADINA *and* PAULINA *have put up a card-table in the centre of the room;* SHAMRAEFF *lights the candles and arranges the chairs, then fetches a box of lotto from the cupboard.*

TRIGORIN. The weather has given me a rough welcome. The wind is frightful. If it goes down by morning I shall go fishing in the lake, and shall have a look at the garden and the spot—do you remember?—where your play was given. I remember the piece very well, but should like to see again where the scene was laid.

MASHA. [*To her father*] Father, do please let my husband have a horse. He ought to go home.

SHAMRAEFF. [*Angrily*] A horse to go home with! [*Sternly*] You know the horses have just been to the station. I can't send them out again.

MASHA. But there are other horses. [*Seeing that her father remains silent*] You are impossible!

MEDVIEDENKO. I shall go on foot, Masha.

PAULINA. [*With a sigh*] On foot in this weather? [*She takes a seat at the card-table*] Shall we begin?

MEDVIEDENKO. It is only six miles. Good-bye. [*He kisses his wife's hand*] Good-bye, mother. [*His mother-in-law gives him her hand unwillingly*] I should not have troubled you all, but the baby— [*He bows to every one*] Good-bye.

[*He goes out with an apologetic air.*

SHAMRAEFF.   He will get there all right, he is not a major-general.

PAULINA.   Come, let us begin. Don't let us waste time, we shall soon be called to supper.

SHAMRAEFF, MASHA, *and* DORN *sit down at the card-table.*

ARKADINA.   [*To* TRIGORIN] When the long autumn evenings descend on us we while away the time here by playing lotto. Look at this old set; we used it when our mother played with us as children. Don't you want to take a hand in the game with us until supper time? [*She and* TRIGORIN *sit down at the table*] It is a monotonous game, but it is all right when one gets used to it.

[*She deals three cards to each of the players.*

TREPLIEFF.   [*Looking through the pages of the magazine*] He has read his own story, and hasn't even cut the pages of mine.

He lays the magazine on his desk and goes toward the door on the right, stopping as he passes his mother to give her a kiss.

ARKADINA.   Won't you play, Constantine?

TREPLIEFF.   No, excuse me please, I don't feel like it. I am going to take a turn through the rooms.

[*He goes out.*

MASHA.   Are you all ready? I shall begin: twenty-two.

ARKADINA.   Here it is.

MASHA.   Three.

DORN.   Right.

MASHA.   Have you put down three? Eight. Eighty-one. Ten.

SHAMRAEFF.   Don't go so fast.

ARKADINA.   Could you believe it? I am still dazed by the reception they gave me in Kharkoff.

MASHA.   Thirty-four.

[*The notes of a melancholy waltz are heard.*

ARKADINA.   The students gave me an ovation; they sent me three baskets of flowers, a wreath, and this thing here.

She unclasps a brooch from her breast and lays it on the table.

SHAMRAEFF.   There is something worth while!

MASHA.   Fifty.

DORN.   Fifty, did you say?

ARKADINA.   I wore a perfectly magnificent dress; I am no fool when it comes to clothes.

PAULINA.   Constantine is playing again; the poor boy is sad.

SHAMRAEFF.   He has been severely criticised in the papers.

MASHA.   Seventy-seven.

ARKADINA.   They want to attract attention to him.

TRIGORIN.   He doesn't seem able to make a success, he can't somehow strike the right note. There is an odd vagueness about his writings that sometimes verges on delirium. He has never created a single living character.

MASHA.   Eleven.

ARKADINA.   Are you bored, Peter? [*A pause*] He is asleep.

DORN.   The Councillor is taking a nap.

MASHA.   Seven. Ninety.

TRIGORIN.   Do you think I should write if I lived in such a place as this, on the shore of this lake? Never! I should overcome my passion, and give my life up to the catching of fish.

MASHA.   Twenty-eight.

TRIGORIN.   And if I caught a perch or a bass, what bliss it would be!

DORN.   I have great faith in Constantine. I know there is something in him. He thinks in images; his stories are vivid and full of colour, and always affect me deeply. It is only a pity that he has no definite object in view. He creates impressions, and nothing more, and one cannot go far on impressions alone. Are you glad, madam, that you have an author for a son?

ARKADINA.   Just think, I have never read anything of his; I never have time.

MASHA.   Twenty-six.

TREPLIEFF *comes in quietly and sits down at his table.*

SHAMRAEFF.   [*To* TRIGORIN] We have something here that belongs to you, sir.

TRIGORIN.   What is it?

SHAMRAEFF.   You told me to have the sea gull stuffed that Mr. Constantine killed some time ago.

TRIGORIN.   Did I? [*Thoughtfully*] I don't remember.

MASHA.   Sixty-one. One.

TREPLIEFF *throws open the window and stands listening.*

TREPLIEFF.   How dark the night is! I wonder what makes me so restless.

ARKADINA.   Shut the window, Constantine, there is a draught here.

TREPLIEFF *shuts the window.*

MASHA.   Ninety-eight.

TRIGORIN.   See, my card is full.

ARKADINA.   [*Gaily*] Bravo! Bravo!

SHAMRAEFF.   Bravo!

ARKADINA.   Wherever he goes and whatever he does, that man always has good luck. [*She gets up*] And now, come to supper. Our renowned guest did not have any dinner to-day. We can continue our game later. [*To her son*] Come, Constantine, leave your writing and come to supper.

TREPLIEFF.   I don't want anything to eat, mother; I am not hungry.

ARKADINA.   As you please. [*She wakes* SORIN] Come to supper, Peter. [*She takes* SHAMRAEFF's *arm*] Let me tell you about my reception in Kharkoff.

PAULINA *blows out the candles on the table, then she and* DORN *roll* SORIN's *chair out of the room, and all go out through the door on the left, except* TREPLIEFF, *who is left alone.* TREPLIEFF *prepares to write. He runs his eye over what he has already written.*

TREPLIEFF.   I have talked a great deal about new forms of art, but I feel myself gradually slipping into the beaten track. [*He reads*] "The placard cried it from the wall—a pale face in a frame of dusky hair"—cried—frame—that is stupid. [*He scratches out what he was written*] I shall begin again from the place where my hero is wakened by the noise of the rain, but what follows must go. This description of a moonlight night is long and stilted.

Trigorin has worked out a process of his own, and descriptions are easy for him. He writes that the neck of a broken bottle lying on the bank glittered in the moonlight, and that the shadows lay black under the millwheel. There you have a moonlight night before your eyes, but I speak of the shimmering light, the twinkling stars, the distant sounds of a piano melting into the still and scented air, and the result is abominable. [*A pause*] The conviction is gradually forcing itself upon me that good literature is not a question of forms new or old, but of ideas that must pour freely from the author's heart, without his bothering his head about any forms whatsoever. [*A knock is heard at the window nearest the table*] What was that? [*He looks out of the window*] I can't see anything. [*He opens the glass door and looks out into the garden*] I heard some one run down the steps. [*He calls*] Who is there? [*He goes out, and is heard walking quickly along the terrace. In a few minutes he comes back with* Nina Zarietchnaya] Oh, Nina, Nina!

Nina *lays her head on* Treplieff's *breast and stifles her sobs.*

Treplieff.   [*Deeply moved*] Nina, Nina! It is you—you! I felt you would come; all day my heart has been aching for you. [*He takes off her hat and cloak*] My darling, my beloved has come back to me! We mustn't cry, we mustn't cry.
Nina.   There is some one here.
Treplieff.   No one is here.
Nina.   Lock the door, some one might come.
Treplieff.   No one will come in.
Nina.   I know your mother is here. Lock the door.

Treplieff *locks the door on the right and comes back to* Nina.

Treplieff.   There is no lock on that one. I shall put a chair against it. [*He puts an arm-chair against the door*] Don't be frightened, no one shall come in.
Nina.   [*Gazing intently into his face*] Let me look at you. [*She looks about her*] It is warm and comfortable in here. This used to be a sitting-room. Have I changed much?
Treplieff.   Yes, you have grown thinner, and your eyes are larger than they were. Nina, it seems so strange to see you! Why

didn't you let me go to you? Why didn't you come sooner to me? You have been here nearly a week. I know. I have been several times each day to where you live, and have stood like a beggar beneath your window.

NINA. I was afraid you might hate me. I dream every night that you look at me without recognising me. I have been wandering about on the shores of the lake ever since I came back. I have often been near your house, but I have never had the courage to come in. Let us sit down. [*They sit down*] Let us sit down and talk our hearts out. It is so quiet and warm in here. Do you hear the wind whistling outside? As Turgenieff says, "Happy is he who can sit at night under the roof of his home, who has a warm corner in which to take refuge." I am a sea gull—and yet— no. [*She passes her hand across her forehead*] What was I saying? Oh, yes, Turgenieff. He says, "and God help all houseless wanderers."

[*She sobs.*

TREPLIEFF. Nina! You are crying again, Nina!

NINA. It is all right. I shall feel better after this. I have not cried for two years. I went into the garden last night to see if our old theatre were still standing. I see it is. I wept there for the first time in two years, and my heart grew lighter, and my soul saw more clearly again. See, I am not crying now. [*She takes his hand in hers*] So you are an author now, and I am an actress. We have both been sucked into the whirlpool. My life used to be as happy as a child's; I used to wake singing in the morning; I loved you and dreamt of fame, and what is the reality? To-morrow morning early I must start for Eltz by train in a third-class carriage, with a lot of peasants, and at Eltz the educated trades-people will pursue me with compliments. It is a rough life.

TREPLIEFF. Why are you going to Eltz?

NINA. I have accepted an engagement there for the winter. It is time for me to go.

TREPLIEFF. Nina, I have cursed you, and hated you, and torn up your photograph, and yet I have known every minute of my life that my heart and soul were yours for ever. To cease from loving you is beyond my power. I have suffered continually from the time I lost you and began to write, and my life has been almost unendurable. My youth was suddenly plucked from me then, and I seem now to have lived in this world for ninety years. I have called out to you, I have kissed the ground you walked on, wherever I looked I have seen your face before my eyes, and the smile that had illumined for me the best years of my life.

NINA. [*Despairingly*] Why, why does he talk to me like this?

TREPLIEFF. I am quite alone, unwarmed by any attachment. I am as cold as if I were living in a cave. Whatever I write is dry and gloomy and harsh. Stay here, Nina, I beseech you, or else let me go away with you.

NINA *quickly puts on her coat and hat.*

TREPLIEFF. Nina, why do you do that? For God's sake, Nina!
[*He watches her as she dresses. A pause.*

NINA. My carriage is at the gate. Do not come out to see me off. I shall find the way alone. [*Weeping*] Let me have some water.

TREPLIEFF *hands her a glass of water.*

TREPLIEFF. Where are you going?

NINA. Back to the village. Is your mother here?

TREPLIEFF. Yes, my uncle fell ill on Thursday, and we telegraphed for her to come.

NINA. Why do you say that you have kissed the ground I walked on? You should kill me rather. [*She bends over the table*] I am so tired. If I could only rest—rest. [*She raises her head*] I am a sea gull—no—no, I am an actress. [*She hears* ARKADINA *and* TRIGORIN *laughing in the distance, runs to the door on the left and looks through the keyhole*] He is there too. [*She goes back to* TREPLIEFF] Ah, well—no matter. He does not believe in the theatre; he used to laugh at my dreams, so that little by little I became down-hearted and ceased to believe in it too. Then came all the cares of love, the continual anxiety about my little one, so that I soon grew trivial and spiritless, and played my parts without meaning. I never knew what to do with my hands, and I could not walk properly or control my voice. You cannot imagine the state of mind of one who knows as he goes through a play how terribly badly he is acting. I am a sea gull—no—no, that is not what I meant to say. Do you remember how you shot a sea gull once? A man chanced to pass that way and destroyed it out of idleness. That is an idea of a short story, but it is not what I meant to say. [*She passes her hand across her forehead*] What was I saying? Oh, yes, the stage. I have changed now. Now I am a real actress. I act with joy, with exaltation, I am intoxicated by it, and feel that I am superb. I have been walking and walking, and thinking and thinking, ever since I have been here, and I feel the strength of my spirit growing in me every day. I know now, I understand at last, Constantine, that for us, whether we write or act, it is not the honour and glory of which I have dreamt that is important, it is the strength to endure. One must know how to bear one's cross, and one must have faith. I believe, and so do not suffer so much, and when I think of my calling I do not fear life.

TREPLIEFF. [*Sadly*] You have found your way, you know where you are going, but I am still groping in a chaos of phantoms and dreams, not knowing whom and what end I am serving by it all. I do not believe in anything, and I do not know what my calling is.

NINA. [*Listening*] Hush! I must go. Good-bye. When I have become a famous actress you must come and see me. Will you promise to come? But now— [*She takes his hand*] it is late. I can hardly stand. I am fainting. I am hungry.

TREPLIEFF. Stay, and let me bring you some supper.

NINA. No, no—and don't come out, I can find the way alone. My carriage is not far away. So she brought him back with her? However, what difference can that make to me? Don't tell Trigorin anything when you see him. I love him—I love him even more than I used to. It is an idea for a short story. I love him—I love him passionately—I love him to despair. Have you forgotten, Constantine, how pleasant the old times were? What a gay, bright, gentle, pure life we led? How a feeling as sweet and tender as a flower blossomed in our hearts? Do you remember, [*She recites*] "All men and beasts, lions, eagles, and quails, horned stags, geese, spiders, silent fish that inhabit the waves, starfish from the sea, and creatures invisible to the eye—in one word, life—all, all life, completing the dreary round set before it, has died out at last. A thousand years have passed since the earth last bore a living creature on its breast, and the unhappy moon now lights her lamp in vain. No longer are the cries of storks heard in the meadows, or the drone of beetles in the groves of limes——"

> *She embraces* TREPLIEFF *impetuously and runs out onto the terrace.*

TRÉPLIEFF. [*After a pause*] It would be a pity if she were seen in the garden. My mother would be distressed.

> *He stands for several minutes tearing up his manuscripts and throwing them under the table, then unlocks the door on the right and goes out.*

DORN. [*Trying to force open the door on the left*] Odd! This door seems to be locked. [*He comes in and puts the chair back in its former place*] This is like a hurdle race.

> ARKADINA *and* PAULINA *come in, followed by* JACOB *carrying some bottles; then come* MASHA, SHAMRAEFF, *and* TRIGORIN.

ARKADINA. Put the claret and the beer here, on the table, so that we can drink while we are playing. Sit down, friends.

PAULINA. And bring the tea at once.

> *She lights the candles and takes her seat at the card-table.* SHAMRAEFF *leads* TRIGORIN *to the cupboard.*

SHAMRAEFF. Here is the stuffed sea gull I was telling you about. [*He takes the sea gull out of the cupboard*] You told me to have it done.

TRIGORIN. [*Looking at the bird*] I don't remember a thing about it, not a thing.

> [*A shot is heard. Every one jumps.*

ARKADINA. [*Frightened*] What was that?

DORN. Nothing at all; probably one of my medicine bottles has blown up. Don't worry. [*He goes out through the door on the right, and comes back in a few moments*] It is as I thought, a flask of ether has exploded. [*He sings*]

"Spellbound once more I stand before thee."

ARKADINA. [*Sitting down at the table*] Heavens! I was really frightened. That noise reminded me of— [*She covers her face with her hands*] Everything is black before my eyes.

DORN. [*Looking through the pages of a magazine, to* TRIGORIN] There was an article from America in this magazine about two months ago that I wanted to ask you about, among other things. [*He leads* TRIGORIN *to the front of the stage*] I am very much interested in this question. [*He lowers his voice and whispers*] You must take Madame Arkadina away from here; what I wanted to say was, that Constantine has shot himself.

The curtain falls.